Malala Yousafzai

Education Activist

by Kate Moening

BELLWETHER MEDIA • MINNEAPOLIS, MN

Note to Librarians, Teachers, and Parents:

Blastoff! Readers are carefully developed by literacy experts and combine standards-based content with developmentally appropriate text.

Level 1 provides the most support through repetition of high-frequency words, light text, predictable sentence patterns, and strong visual support.

Level 2 offers early readers a bit more challenge through varied simple sentences, increased text load, and less repetition of high-frequency words.

Level 3 advances early-fluent readers toward fluency through increased text and concept load, less reliance on visuals, longer sentences, and more literary language.

Level 4 builds reading stamina by providing more text per page, increased use of punctuation, greater variation in sentence patterns, and increasingly challenging vocabulary.

Level 5 encourages children to move from "learning to read" to "reading to learn" by providing even more text, varied writing styles, and less familiar topics.

Whichever book is right for your reader, Blastoff! Readers are the perfect books to build confidence and encourage a love of reading that will last a lifetime!

This edition first published in 2020 by Bellwether Media, Inc.

No part of this publication may be reproduced in whole or in part without written permission of the publisher. For information regarding permission, write to Bellwether Media, Inc., Attention: Permissions Department, 6012 Blue Circle Drive, Minnetonka, MN 55343.

Library of Congress Cataloging-in-Publication Data

Names: Moening, Kate, author.
Title: Malala Yousafzai : Education Activist / by Kate Moening.
Description: Minneapolis, MN : Bellwether Media, Inc., [2020] | Series: Blastoff! Readers : Women Leading the Way | Audience: Ages 5-8. | Audience: Grades K-3. | Includes bibliographical references and index.
Identifiers: LCCN 2018053345 (print) | LCCN 2019008301 (ebook) | ISBN 9781618916730 (ebook) | ISBN 9781644871010 (hardcover : alk. paper) | ISBN 9781618917249 (pbk. : alk. paper)
Subjects: LCSH: Yousafzai, Malala, 1997- | Women social reformers–Pakistan–Biography–Juvenile literature. | Women political activists–Pakistan–Biography–Juvenile literature. | Girls–Education–Pakistan–Juvenile literature.
Classification: LCC LC2330 (ebook) | LCC LC2330 .M64 2020 (print) | DDC 370.82095491–dc23
LC record available at https://lccn.loc.gov/2018053345

Editor: Al Albertson   Designer: Andrea Schneider

Printed in the United States of America, North Mankato, MN.

Table of Contents

Who Is Malala Yousafzai?

Malala Yousafzai is an **activist**. She fights for girls' **education**.

In many places, girls cannot go to school. Malala especially fights for them.

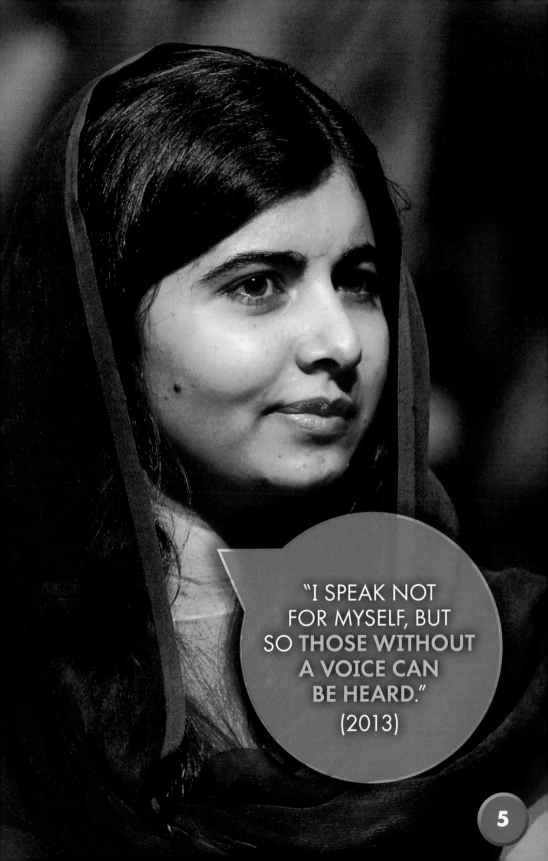

"I SPEAK NOT FOR MYSELF, BUT SO THOSE WITHOUT A VOICE CAN BE HEARD." (2013)

Getting Her Start

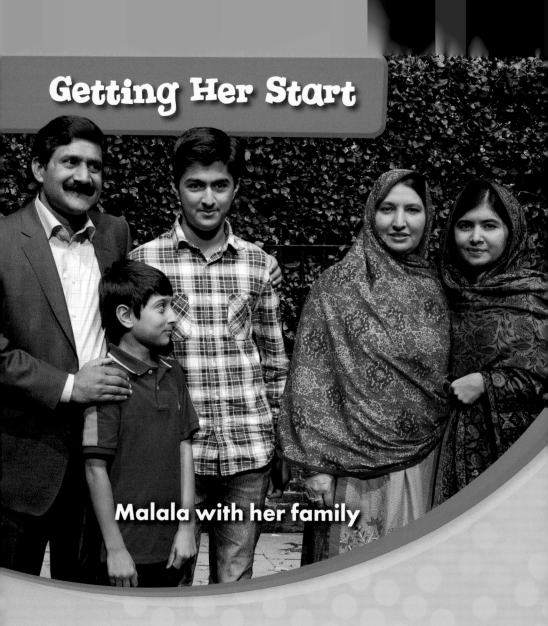

Malala with her family

Malala was born in Pakistan.
She was a curious student.
She played soccer with
her brothers.

At night, Malala's dad
read poetry to his children.

Pakistan

Mingora, Pakistan
Malala's hometown

N
W E
S

Many people in Pakistan thought girls did not need an education.

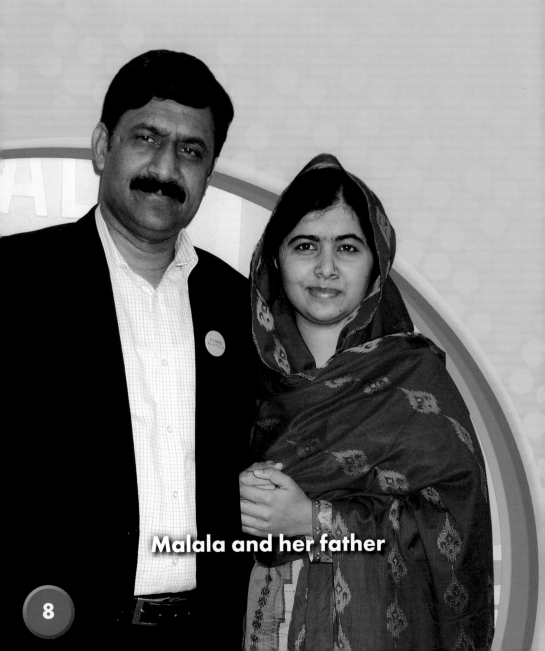

Malala and her father

Malala Yousafzai Profile

Birthday: July 12, 1997

Industries:
education and activism

Hometown:
Mingora, Pakistan

Education:
- studying politics, philosophy, and economics (University of Oxford)

Influences and Heroes:
- Ziauddin Yousafzai (father)
- Toor Pekai Yousafzai (mother)
- Martin Luther King, Jr. (activist; minister)
- Nelson Mandela (activist; former president of South Africa)
- Emma Watson (actress)

But Malala's dad ran a school. He wanted Malala to learn!

When Malala was 11, the **Taliban** took over. They destroyed many girls' schools.

Malala fought back. She wrote a **blog** for a news **company**. She spoke about girls' education on television.

girls' school in Pakistan

Malala speaking live on German television

Changing the World

Malala near her hometown after being shot

The Taliban did not like Malala speaking out. One day, they got on her school bus. They shot her!

Malala went to England to **heal**.

people praying for Malala

Malala kept fighting.
She knew education
could give girls
a better future.

Malala wrote a book!
She also started the
Malala **Fund**.

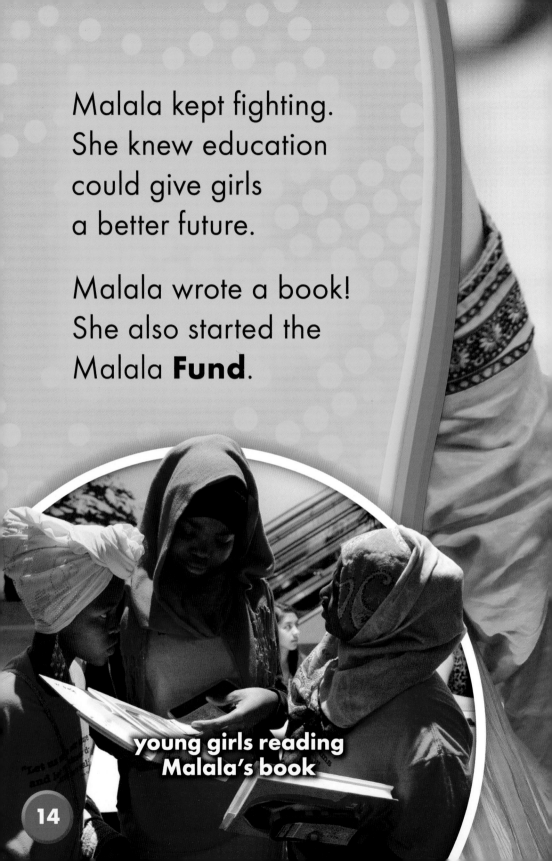

**young girls reading
Malala's book**

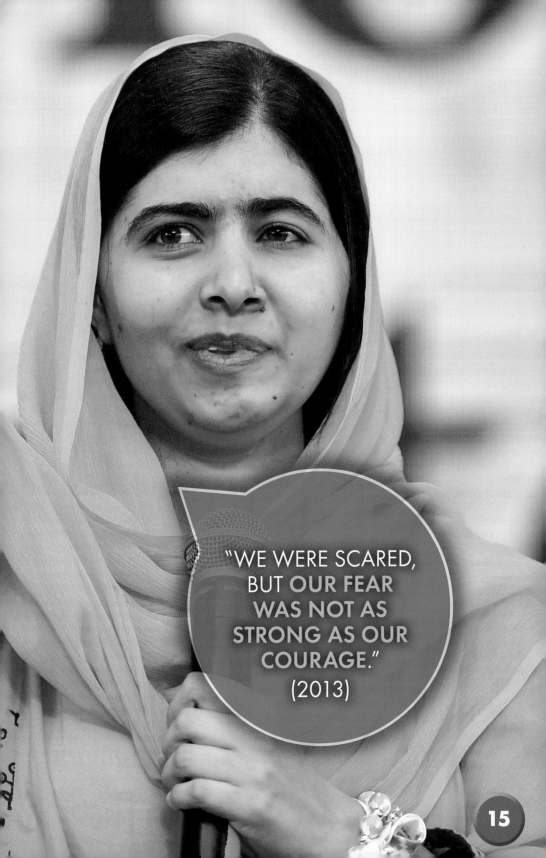

"WE WERE SCARED, BUT OUR FEAR WAS NOT AS STRONG AS OUR COURAGE." (2013)

**Malala with former president
Barack Obama**

Malala speaks with many world
leaders. She says education can
stop wars and help poor countries.

Malala won an **award** for her peaceful work.

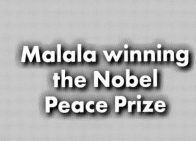

Malala winning the Nobel Peace Prize

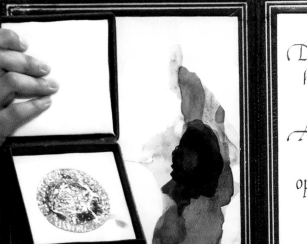

Den Norske Nobelkomite har overensstemmende med reglene i det av

ALFRED NOBEL

den 27. november 1895 opprettede testamente tildelt

Malala Yousafzai

Nobels Fredspris

Malala's Future

Today, Malala is in college!

Malala Yousafzai Timeline

2009	Malala starts blogging for the British Broadcasting Company
2012	Malala is shot by the Taliban
2013	Malala starts the Malala Fund to help children around the world go to school
2014	Malala wins the Nobel Peace Prize
2017	Malala starts college

She believes education is a **human right**. She keeps fighting.

Malala travels to many countries where girls still cannot go to school.

Malala wants everyone to use their voice. She believes every person can change the world!

"ONE CHILD, ONE TEACHER, ONE BOOK, ONE PEN CAN **CHANGE THE WORLD**." (2013)

Glossary

activist—a person who believes in taking action to make changes in laws or society

award—a reward or prize that is given for a job well done

blog—a web site on which someone writes about personal opinions, activities, and experiences

company—a group that makes, buys, or sells goods for money

education—the knowledge, skill, and understanding that a person gets from going to school

fund—an organization that gives money to a special cause

heal—to become healthy or well again

human right—something that every person should be allowed to have, get, or do

Taliban—a group in Pakistan that uses violence to gain power

To Learn More

AT THE LIBRARY

Duling, Kaitlyn. *Malala Yousafzai*. Minneapolis, Minn.: Jump!, Inc., 2019.

Halligan, Katherine. *HerStory: 50 Girls and Women Who Shook Up the World*. New York, N.Y.: Simon & Schuster Books for Young Readers, 2018.

Yousafzai, Malala. *Malala's Magic Pencil*. New York, N.Y.: Little, Brown and Company, 2017.

ON THE WEB

FACTSURFER

Factsurfer.com gives you a safe, fun way to find more information.

1. Go to www.factsurfer.com.

2. Enter "Malala Yousafzai" into the search box and click 🔍.

3. Select your book cover to see a list of related web sites.

Index